Friends 4 Ever

The New You!

||||| W9-AZR-588

Slumber-ific!

Great Sleepover Ideas for You and Your Friends

For best friends everywhere.

—J.H.

For Alison, every girl needs a sister like you.

—T.M.

ISBN-13: 978-0-439-02015-2
ISBN-10: 0-439-02015-8

12 11 10 9 8   14 15 16 17/0

Printed in the U.S.A.
First printing, September 2007

Friends **4** Ever

The New You!

Slumber-ific!

Great Sleepover Ideas for You and Your Friends

by Jo Hurley
Illustrated by Taia Morley

Scholastic Inc.
New York   Toronto   London   Auckland   Sydney
Mexico City   New Delhi   Hong Kong   Buenos Aires

Rachel

Name: Rachel

Nickname: Red

Pet: Cat   **Hair:** Wavy

Favorite Thing to Read: Comic books

Favorite Person at School: Drama teacher

Favorite Article of Clothing: Peasant skirt

Best Dream: Win Academy Award

Worst Nightmare: Stage fright

Sam

Name: Samantha

Nickname: Sam

Pet: Dog   **Hair:** Bangs

Favorite Thing to Read: Sports stats

Favorite Person at School: Coach

Favorite Article of Clothing: Jean jacket

Best Dream: Olympic champion

Worst Nightmare: Broken leg

JESSIE

Name: Jessica

Nickname: Jessie

Pet: Turtle   **Hair:** Ponytail

Favorite Thing to Read: Anything!

Favorite Person at School: Librarian

Favorite Article of Clothing: Sweater set

Best Dream: Write a novel

Worst Nightmare: Computer crash

Name: Elizabeth

Nickname: Libby

Pet: Guinea pig   **Hair:** Curls

Favorite Thing to Read: Teen magazines

Favorite Person at School: All my BFFs

Favorite Article of Clothing: Can't pick just one!

Best Dream: Helping a charitable cause

Worst Nightmare: Bad hair day

Libby

Sweet Dreams

If you and your friends are like the friends 4-ever, then you hang out at school, after school, and on the weekends. You can be seen shopping at the mall, studying in the school library, or shooting hoops at the park. But the best, best, BEST place to get together is the ultimate friend fest: the slumber party.

I'VE GOT MY SOFT PILLOW AND SLEEPING BAG READY TO GO.

Wait! We're not going to sleep, are we?

Looking for ideas? Oooh! There are so many ways to make *your* party simply slumber-ific—and we're here to help!

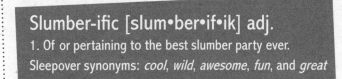

Slumber-ific [slum•ber•if•ik] adj.
1. Of or pertaining to the best slumber party ever.
Sleepover synonyms: *cool*, *wild*, *awesome*, *fun*, and *great*

Not me! I want to stay up and have fun!

Yeah, if we snooze, we lose....

Get It Together

Every great slumber party needs a great slumber party plan. We've got some ideas (based on our party experiences) that just might help. Give yourself at least three weeks to put your plan into action.

You Are Cordially Invited

How will you let everyone know about your big bash? A perfect invitation is the first way to get your pals excited about the event.

Use your invitation to present your party theme. Throughout the book, we've included different invitation ideas based on themes we love.

Include all the important information: your name, the theme of the party (if there is one), the party location, the date and time when the party starts, and the finishing time (so guests can plan pickups the following day).

Include an RSVP with a phone number and deadline when you need to hear back.

Who's Who

Once you've decided upon a theme for the party, it's time to make your guest list. After all, you have to send out those invitations—pronto! Making a list of invitees is sometimes a hard task. You can't invite everyone you know, but you don't want to leave anyone out or hurt anyone's feelings.

A good rule for sleepovers: Keep the guest count *low*. The best slumber parties are ones that have a small number of close friends.

Remember: You'll be with one another for a long time.

Did you know RSVP means "Répondez S'il Vous Plaît"? That's French for "respond, if you please."

Jessie Knows!

To Sleep or Not to Sleep?

(That is TOTALLY the question!)

To me, the best part of any sleepover is the food. I like it when the party hostess puts out a smorgasbord of snacks. My tummy's grumbling just thinking about it....

No slumber party is complete without a mascot. Although my friends laugh at me, I never go anywhere without mr. Bear.

THE FIRST TIME I EVER SLEPT OVER AT A FRIEND'S HOUSE, THE POWER WENT OUT. WE SPENT THE WHOLE TIME TELLING GHOST STORIES.

One time, I had a sleepover at my house. I made a list of all these things to do but we ended up spending the entire party gossiping.

What's Cooking?

One of the real secrets to a slumber party's success is the food! You need dinner, snacks, *and* don't forget—breakfast!

Get an adult to help you make a sleepover shopping list. Check out the individual party themes on pages 15 to 51 for suggested party recipes and snacks.

The Ultimate Sleepover Breakfast

Happy Face Pancakes

★ Raisins and banana slices for eyes

★ Apple slice for smile

★ Cut banana for ears

★ Strawberry slice for nose

★ Drizzle syrup for hairdo

I always ate these as a little kid! Use your favorite pancake mix and decorate away!

Other quick and easy breakfast ideas:

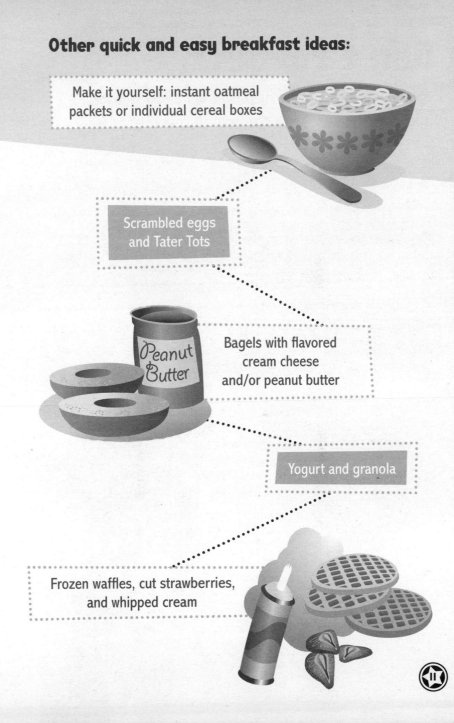

Make it yourself: instant oatmeal packets or individual cereal boxes

Scrambled eggs and Tater Tots

Peanut Butter

Bagels with flavored cream cheese and/or peanut butter

Yogurt and granola

Frozen waffles, cut strawberries, and whipped cream

Don't Forget!

There's more to party planning than games and food. There's sleepover etiquette, too!

In addition to a sleepover setup plan, you need a cleanup plan. Don't leave a big mess for your parents to pick up. Keep the house neat as you go.

Heads up: No sleeping on sofas or beds. That way you can't fight over them! Put your sleeping bags on the floor in a starburst position, with everyone's heads facing into the center of the circle.

No punking or pranking allowed! Although slumber parties are sometimes known for their silly pranks and practical jokes, you don't have to indulge. No one wants hurt feelings. Keep *your* party fair and fun.

Got manners? When the party's over, always, always send a thank-you note if your guests brought a gift. On the flip side, it's a nice idea to send a thank-you note after you attend a slumber party, too.

I thought parties for my best pals meant that I didn't need to worry about thank-you cards. But now I realize that good friends are the ones who deserve a thank you most of all.

Chaperone Alert!

Of course you'll need a chaperone for your party. But who wants to spend the entire night worried that Mom or Dad will walk in and crash your bash? Here's an easy fix: Before guests arrive, set guidelines with your parents and other members of your household. Establish how often they will check on you during the party.

Just when I thought my little sister would invade my sleepover, Dad whisked her away to the movies. That was so cool! She wasn't around to pester us all night.

Slumber Party Checklist

I LIKE BEING ORGANIZED ABOUT MY PARTIES! THIS IS THE CHECKLIST I ALWAYS USE. YOU CAN USE IT, TOO! DID I FORGET ANYTHING?

Pick theme ☐ ⋯⋯ Time & date ☐ ⋯

Choose location ☐ ⋯ ☐ Make (buy) invites ⋯ ☐ Make guest list

⋯ Choose (borrow, download) music ☐ ⋯⋯ Mail invites ☐ ⋯

☐ Plan menu ⋯ ☐ Purchase supplies ⋯ ☐ Fix up/overhaul bedroom

☐ Make decorations ☐ ⋯⋯ Make room for sleeping bags ☐ ⋯

☐ Have fun! ⋯⋯

New & Improved
Party Checklist
by Rachel & Sam

Wait! You almost forgot some very important things to do....

☐ Stock up on camera and film (funny or not, you'll want to remember *these* party friends 4-ever)

☐ Make a list of all-important pillow fight rules (whatever's clever)

☐ Plan alternative menu (all chocolate, all the time)

Pick a Theme, Any Theme

At the core of every great slumber party is a great theme. And it doesn't matter if your theme is sports or beauty salon—as long as you stick to it!

Invitations?

Party Favors?

Things to Do?

What to Wear?

WHAT TO EAT?

What to Bring?

Turn the page for the best sleepover themes ever....

Theme: Hooray for Hollywood

Let's have a superstar sleepover complete with paparazzi!

Party Mantra:

GLAM, I AM

Libby

Invitation Ideas: Party Doll

····················· You need: ····················

cardstock • glitter glue • colored paper • tissue paper • yarn
stick-on googly eyes • regular white glue • scissors • markers

What to Do:

 Draw the shape of a girl's body onto the cardstock. (You're making a paper doll, so make the figure about 8 inches high.) Then cut it out.

 Decorate the top of the head with yarn (for hair), add googly eyes, and draw a mouth and nose.

 Cut out pieces of colored paper and tissue paper to make a shirt, shorts, or a dress (however you want to dress your doll!).

Ⓐ On the back of the paper doll, write the invitation instructions. *You're invited to GET GLAM at a real Hollywood sleepover....*

Make a replica of the Hollywood sign! Cut out the words "Hooray for HOLLYWOOD" (with one word in capital letters just like the sign) from a piece of white cardstock. Place them onto a piece of green felt. Decorate the felt border with glitter glue stripes or dots or little star shapes. On the back of the felt, glue another square piece of cardstock with all the party details.

Wanted: Glam Girls

You're off to a Hollywood party, but you've got a looong way to go before you feel truly glamorous? Don't worry! Help is just a makeover away....

FIRST: Get the right clothes. For this party, you'll need fancy pj's or nightgowns plus a few other flashy pieces like silver or gold (fake) jewelry, a rhinestone tiara, wigs, and "dressy" shoes (or fluffy slippers).

SECOND: Get the right name. You'll hit a "glam slam" with the right fake Hollywood name. Check out the chart below. Keep your first name but change your last name. Use the first letter of your first name to find the substitute glam last name. For example, if your name is Laura, your new glam name would be Laura Luster. If you were Sydney, you'd be Sydney Superglam.

A Awesome	H Hushabye	N Nicely	U Unstoppable
B Buttercup	I Idol	O Ooh-la-la	V Victory
C Charming	J Joy	P Precious	W Whisper
D Diamond	K Kingdom	Q Queenie	X X-tra
E Elegance	L Luster	R Ravishing	Y Youthful
F Feathers	M Megabucks	S Superglam	Z Zip Zap
G Glitter		T Tickles	

Lights, Camera, Showtime

What would a Hollywood party be without movies? Plan to show a few glam flicks featuring your favorite screen princesses and girly-girls. A few suggestions:

•Princess Diaries • The Princess Bride • A Cinderella Story • Confessions of a Teenage Drama Queen

Swap and Strut

Make a Hollywood glamour catwalk—complete with models, attitude, and borrowed clothes. Collect a variety of glamorous clothes. You can borrow from your mom or use old Halloween costumes. Put them into a single pile in the middle of the room. Set a timer and say, "Go!" In that time, every girl has to grab at least two items—and model those clothes on a runway or a red carpet (just like a movie premiere). Take pictures with a digital camera and everyone can have a memento to bring home!

Guess the Star

You need:
scraps of paper • marker • masking tape

What to do: Give each girl at the party a piece of paper, a marker, and a piece of tape. Each girl needs to write down the name of a famous starlet. Then take the paper and stick it on the back of another glam guest (without her seeing the name). During the course of the game, everyone asks questions to guess the identity of her own mystery starlet.

Good Eats

How do you get glam food? Take something ordinary and make it extraordinary. Why not make very special popcorn munchies to go with your princess movies? Pop some kernels in the microwave or on the stovetop (with help from an adult). When the popcorn is popped, add in funky food and flavorings your guests will love.

Pizza, pizza! Pour melted butter over the warm popcorn. Then sprinkle on a little pizza seasoning and Parmesan cheese.

Cinnamon and sugar
(combined *before* putting onto the popcorn)

Raisins, corn Chex, peanuts, little pretzels

Party Treats

Give each of your guests a truly glamorous goody bag. You could include:

Mini-tubes of lip gloss

Disposable cameras
(that's the paparazzi part)

Plastic sunglasses in bright colors like pink and purple

Mini-notebooks (for autographs)

Party Plan:

Plan a tropical survival party (yes, like the TV show) with games and dares. The only things missing will be the bug bites and sunburns!

Invitation Ideas

Use kraft paper to write out your invitation instructions. Then roll up the paper into a scroll and tie it with raffia or twine.

Draw a tiki/totem pole onto colored paper and write party details up the side.

Give your party an imaginary desert island locale and write "Who will SURVIVE this party?"

Fashion Statement

Look the part: Wear fatigues, comfy T-shirts, and shorts that give you that "desert island/jungle" look. Or, provide colorful T-shirts to all party guests. At some point early on in the party, have guests invent a *Survivor*-like team name and design a logo for their shirts.

Your Challenge, Should You Choose to Accept It...

Some of these activities work best outdoors!

Host a gummy critter eating contest. You can find Gummy Worms or Gummy Frogs at most supermarkets or candy stores. Open wide and just pretend they're real. Gross!

Be a puzzle maniac! On the TV show Survivor, the cast has to solve assorted puzzles to win prizes. You can do the same thing. Make copies of an easy word search or crossword puzzle. See who can finish it the fastest.

It's a junk hunt! Make a list of random objects for everyone to find and/or identify. You can do this in your basement, bedroom, or even outdoors.

Water, water! Teams carry cups filled with water from a starting line to fill a bucket 5-10 feet away. There's one hitch: The cups have little holes and are leaking. Outdoor activity, please!

Can you do the tree stump stand? See who can balance the longest on one foot. If you have a stump or sturdy chair to stand on that works best, but you can also just stand in place to do it.

Good Eats

Eeeew! Gross!

Dirt and Worms

You Need:

- 8 inch pot or bowl

- Large package of Oreo cookies

- 12 oz. container Cool Whip
  (or other whipped topping)

- 2 packages instant
  pudding–vanilla or chocolate

- 1 package (or 1/2 pound)
  Gummy Worms

What to Do:

 Crush Oreo cookies and set aside.

 Combine pudding and cookies, leaving some cookie crumbs aside.

 Fold Cool Whip into the mix.

 Take pot or bowl and begin to layer your ingredients. Start with a bottom layer of Oreo crumbs. Then add a layer of the wet mixture. Then add a layer of Gummy Worms. Continue until the pot is filled. Place a final layer of cookie crumbs on top.

Keep in the refrigerator overnight. Serve cold.

Party Treats

Get creative with prizes for your various challenges. Give away rubber snakes, tiki necklaces, or cool whistles. The morning after your sleepover, pass out "We Had a Ball" beach balls for everyone to inflate and sign with permanent marker. They make great mementos for your party!

Theme: Mega Magic

I CAN'T DECIDE ON MY FAVORITE MAGICIAN: HARRY HOUDINI OR HARRY POTTER?

Jessie

PARTY GOAL: TO MAKE EVERYONE DISAPPEAR!
JUST KIDDING!

Invitation Ideas

Try this!
Use colored paper, glue, and silver glitter to make a medium-sized top hat with the hat on one side and a white rabbit on the opposite side. You can even glue a cotton ball on for a rabbit tail. Write invitation details on the hat side. A good opening line: "The rabbit is about to come out of the hat...."

The rabbit is about to come out of the hat!

Or try this!
Roll a piece of 8 1/2 x 11-inch construction paper into a tube and tape together. This is your magic wand. Decorate the outside with paint and stickers. Put invitation details onto a separate sheet of paper. Photocopy the paper, roll up, and slip inside each wand, and staple the ends together. For added magic, toss in a handful of metallic confetti pieces into the wand, too.

Fashion Statement
A cape with gold stars and a cone-shaped wizard hat! What else?

Party Activities and Games

A mega-magic party should probably have a mega-magic showtime (with you or your friends performing easy tricks). But there are other games you can play, too.

Put out arts and crafts supplies and ask guests to decorate a magician's hat.

Play Disappearing Guest, otherwise known as plain old hide-and-seek.

Go on a magical treasure hunt to find hidden objects in your house or yard. Make it even more interesting by writing clues with invisible ink pens, simple riddles, or backward handwriting.

Turn Left.

Just before it's time for lights-out, play the Sleeping Bag Guessing Game. Pick one girl to leave the room. She'll be the guesser. When she's gone, everyone should mix up sleeping bags, get inside, and zip up. When the guesser comes back into the room, she should walk around and find creative ways of identifying who is zipped into each bag. Try tickling the bags. It works great!

E-Z Magic Tricks You and Your Friends Can Perform

Shell game

Coin tricks

Simple card tricks

Make Your Own Invisible Ink

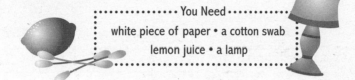

•••••••••••• You Need ••••••••••
white piece of paper • a cotton swab
lemon juice • a lamp

What to Do:

Simply dip the swab into lemon juice and write your message onto the paper. It will dry clear BUT when you hold the page up to a light source (being very careful not to ignite the paper), the message will appear.

Now THAT's MAGIC!

Good Eats

WHAT'S A MAGIC PARTY WITHOUT A
BATCH OF WIZARD HAT CUPCAKES? MAKE THESE AND PRESTO! YOU'LL BE AMAZED AT HOW SWEET YOUR GUESTS WILL FEEL. . . .

Bake (or purchase) two dozen cupcakes (any flavor). Thinly frost with your favorite color icing . . . and then stop. Party guests will do the rest!

Place the following out onto a tablecloth: cupcakes, at least one package of sugar ice-cream cones, extra frosting (in different colors), Cool Whip or other whipped topping, colored sugars, colored sprinkles, and other add-on confections that you can find in the supermarket baking aisle.

Have guests place a cone onto each frosted cupcake and decorate the cone (now a wizard's hat!) with frosting, whipped topping, and more. Make it sparkle!

Party Treats

When assembling goody bags, look for bargains. Dollar stores, Oriental Trading Company, and other novelty shops let you purchase lots of goodies for less money. Some of the magical items you could buy cheaply may include:

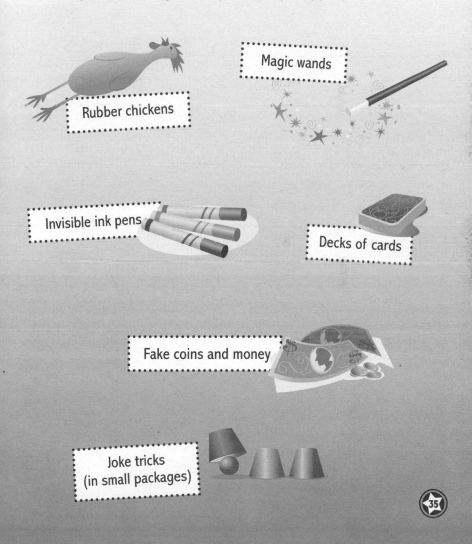

Magic wands

Rubber chickens

Invisible ink pens

Decks of cards

Fake coins and money

Joke tricks
(in small packages)

Theme: Beauty Break

No sleepover is complete
without a makeover!
My goal: to feel beautiful
outside and inside!

Libby

Invitation Ideas

Cut out paper and design the invitation in the shape of a flower.

Make a paper invitation that looks like a sign at the front of a real beauty shop: PLEASE ENTER. Use glitter glue and puffy paint to make words and doodles pop off the front. Inside the envelope of each invite, place a temporary heart or flower tattoo for guests.

Before guests arrive, set the spa scene. Light candles. Serve water with lemon. Play music. Be sure to have towels and washcloths on hand, too.

Fashion Statement

If this were a real spa, you'd be dressed in a comfy robe with flip-flops, so why don't you do the same for your party? A T-shirt, sweatpants, and slip-ons work just as well. Ask your friends to bring their robes or other comfy clothes.

You may be queen for a day—but you can't just sit there! Play a few games and have fun getting beautiful.

Makeup Madness

Each party guest gets a small tray of basic makeup: eye shadow, lipstick, powder, etc. The party host sets a timer as all guests are given one minute to apply makeup to their own faces without looking in a mirror. A variation on this game is to do it in pairs. One girl must be blindfolded as she applies makeup to her friend's face—with funny results.

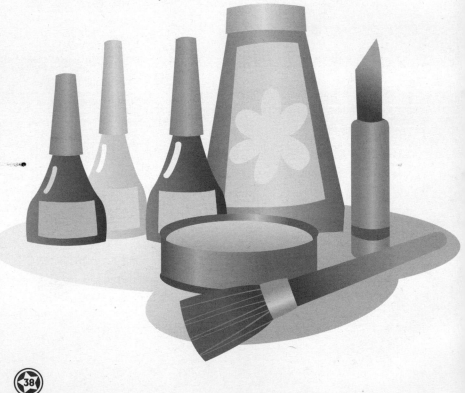

Cosmetics Hide-and-Seek

Purchase small cosmetic samples at the discount drugstore. Hide them throughout your home. Give each guest a few minutes to locate as many as possible.

Spa Treatment Switcheroo

Set up beauty "stations" (one for nails, one for makeup, one for hair, etc.). Have girls travel from station to station. Don't forget to have instant or digital cameras on hand to capture the before and after photos for each girl.

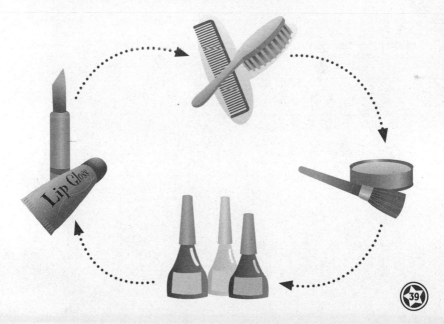

Make It!
Body Glitter

What to Do:

1 Each girl should design a label for her cosmetic container. Can you think of a fun name for your homemade body glitter?

2 Fill the container about half to three-quarters full with the gel.

3 Sprinkle the glitter into the gel and mix with wooden craft sticks. Voilà!

Good Eats

Type up special menus (like the ones they present in actual spas).

Give 'em creative names like Berry Blast-off and Pineapple Perfection when you add strawberries or tropical fruit.

MMM MMM FRUIT SMOOTHIES

SUPER SALAD

HOMEMADE GRANOLA

Starring the usual lettuce and tomato—plus other interesting add-ons like sunflower seeds, dried cranberries or raisins, and more.

Any healthy munchies will do!

Party Treats

No beauty sleepover grab bag would be complete without:

Hair clips or ribbons

Scented bubble bath

BUBBLE BATH

Mini-loofahs

Mini-soaps

SOAP

Theme: American Idol

Sing out, sister!

Rachel

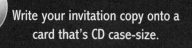

Write your invitation copy onto a card that's CD case-size.

Use blue and silver paper for a mod-looking invitation.

Cut out the silhouette of a microphone or a musical note.

Fashion Statement

Give yourself and guests the regal pop star treatment. That means feather boas, glitter sunglasses, tons of cool (and fake) jewelry, and different-sized hats (and more).

Think Outside the Box!

If singing isn't exactly your thing but you like to perform in other ways, you can adjust your party theme. There are so many reality TV shows that would work as sleepover party themes. Like...what about So You Think You Can Dance? Can *you* dance?

Party Activities and Games

It's the best singing contest ever—starring you and your buddies!

 Everyone picks a tune to sing. Limit preparation time to 15 minutes so you spend more time performing.

Have volunteers like Mom, an older brother, or even another friend do the judging, or make the judging fun. Here's how: Take scraps of paper and write down random compliments on the pieces like "You rocked!" or "Loved your song choice." Fill a bowl with these slips of paper. Each time someone new performs, select one of the scraps as a critique. This is a good way to give everyone compliments—and keep spirits high throughout the party.

Feel the Beat

Rent a karaoke machine and take turns belting out tunes.

Pretend you've just been signed to a major record label. Now design your very first CD cover. Give it a name, create a logo, and add funky art.

String up little white lights from the ceiling or on the wall to suggest a stage area.

Turn on the radio so you can identify songs from their opening bars of music. The first guest to correctly ID three songs in a row wins a prize.

Good Eats

What do all the big stars eat and drink in their concert dressing rooms? Many have their favorite foods like ziti or hamburgers or hummus—but some stars make funny (and strange) requests like "one bowl of green M&M's." What would be your special request?

> Imagine trading places with Cristina, Mariah, or Kelly for just one day. What would your concert dates and destinations be?

Sound Off!

Sit around with your BFFs and make a list of all the cool songs you'd put on your ultimate soundtrack.

_____

_____

_____

_____

_____

_____

_____

Party Treats

Hand out copies of a CD-mix that you made yourself.

Give everyone a feather boa or a star necklace.

Theme: The Big Game

Batter up!

Samantha

Invitation Ideas

Cut out shapes of different sports equipment like footballs, soccer balls, or tennis racquets. Write party details on the front side. Use cute sports lingo to grab the attention of the person reading the invitation. For example, "Hey! Party Time! Let's Have a Ball!" Or, "Kick It with Your Friends at a Groovy Sports Sleepover."

Send each party invitee a colored bandanna with a card attached that tells the guest a team color along with the time, date, and location of the party.

Design a colored paper invitation with a picture of the five Olympic rings on the front side. Tell friends you're hosting the Party Olympics.

Fashion Statement

The sports party hostess looks best in sports attire. Everyone else can dress the same, sweatbands and all! Maybe Mom or Dad will be a really good sport... and dress up as a referee. Perfect!

Party Activities and Games

Give out POINTS as rewards to winners. . . .

Then offer gold, silver, and bronze medals!

Balloon Volleyball. Divide into teams. Each team stands in a circle and attempts to keep a balloon off the ground for as long as possible. For every minute a team keeps the balloon afloat, that team is given a point.

Long Jump. Mark an "X" on the floor with masking tape. Ask each guest to jump from the starting line. But no running! The longest jump wins points for the team.

Hoop Shoot. Place a garbage can or laundry basket six to eight feet away from a start line that has been marked on the floor with masking tape. Using a spongy, smaller ball, attempt to shoot hoops. Award points for every basket.

Set up an obstacle course around the backyard using cones, tires, and lawn chairs — whatever you have on hand!

Good Eats

A basic sheet cake can be decorated and turned into all kinds of sporting places: a football field, tennis court, basketball court, or swimming pool. Get creative with colored frosting. Add on goal posts with pretzel sticks held together with more frosting.

Have a table out during the party with sports-themed snacks: Gatorade sports drink, water bottles, orange slices, or granola bars should set the scene perfectly.

Party Treats

Spongy balls

Ball and jacks

Sneaker laces

Little plastic whistles in the shape of baseball or soccer ball

Frisbees

Terry cloth wristband

Theme: Making History

I THINK EVERY SLEEPOVER NEEDS TO BE AN ADVENTURE. GRAB YOUR FLASHLIGHTS AND LET'S GO!

Jessie

Invitation Ideas

Find an interesting rock, pine cone, or leaf and do a crayon rubbing. It gives the outside of your invitation an archaeologist feel, like you've taken a rubbing of an actual fossil.

Get fake papyrus, which is Egyptian paper. Make it look older than it is by tearing the edges. You could turn your invitation into a treasure map, too.

Get plain cardstock in a bold color. Then write your entire message in hieroglyphs. The real catch is: The hieroglyphic doodles are made-up by you. Then provide a "cheat sheet" alphabet for the doodles so everyone knows what she's reading.

Fashion Statement

Does anyone have a pith helmet? That's the best kind for exploring. Any other straw hat will do, however. Just don't forget these other accessories for your time-traveling, explorer sleepover. You may want to provide some of these for your guests.

Notebook

Magnifying glass

Compass

Party Activities and Games

Select the time period from history that you'd like to explore the most.

Time After Time

- Ancient Egypt
- Aztecs
- On the *Titanic*
- Vikings
- Ancient Greece

Pretend to be scientists and expedition teams. Make up new names for yourselves and fake names for the expedition like Professor Slither, Snake, and Serpent Research Team.

If you're going on an ancient Egyptian exploration, then play Wrap Your Team Leader in Toilet Paper (kind of like a mummy).

If you're looking at Aztec history, then play Search for the Missing Treasure. Place a bunch of trinkets and/or treasures on a tray. Let your guests study them. Then without them looking, remove a few of the items. Now what's missing?

Organize a scavenger hunt. A great thing to look for: rubber snakes—just like in the jungle. Whoever finds the most snakes wins a prize. Maybe a book? Jessie would love that prize.

Surf the Internet for more ideas tied-in to your theme.

Show a flick that reflects your party's chosen time period. What about Indiana Jones? Or everyone's favorite romantic saga, Titanic? Don't forget the tissues!

Good Eats

Surprise cookies! Bake a batch of sugar cookies (or ask Mom or Dad to do it). But before baking each cookie, insert a slip of paper with a number on it. That number corresponds to a special party prize. It's like a treasure hunt inside a cookie.

Around-the-world menu! If you're time-traveling, you're also visiting different locations around the globe, right? Let your sleepover food selection reflect that. Try serving a multicultural menu: Miniature beef tacos, hummus and pita chips, sliced ham and brie on croissants, and pot sticker dumplings are just a few of the finger foods your guests can taste.

Party Treats

You may want to flip things around a bit for this party. Give your goody bags first. The items inside (like binoculars or a compass) can be used during the party activities. Other stuff to include: a cool pen, a pouch for carrying all your stuff, or a disposable camera for tracking "evidence" during a treasure hunt.

Theme: Art Attack

When I see paint...
I just can't help myself!

Rachel

Invitation Ideas

Cutout palette or easel with small paintbrush attached

Make up a standard invitation card on paper that you decorate yourself—but frame it in a small wooden frame. You can purchase these in most craft stores. For an extra-creative touch, mail the invitation with a tiny package of watercolor paints and a note attached that says: "Can't wait to paint with you!"

Party Activities and Games

The most essential things you need to have at any arts and crafts party are supplies. Stock up on everything from crayons, paint, and glue to sequins, feathers, and Popsicle sticks. And don't forget to supply an apron for each guest. It may be a casual slumber party but no one wants to get paint on their pj's, right? Other stuff to do:

Make a pom-pom boa using multicolored pom-poms and a length of embroidery thread. You need to get a needle (ask Mom or Dad for help with this one). Thread the needle and pull each pom-pom through, linking them together like a long necklace.

Play Art Freeze. Set up at least three art stations (maybe one is crayon coloring, one is painting, and one is glitter glue). Play music as girls float from one station to the next, stopping only when the word FREEZE is called out. Since projects will be interrupted midstream, the next group must continue what's been begun.

Play Pin the Ear on Van Gogh. This is a funny game using a self-portrait of the artist (available in most poster shops). Hang up the poster. Now draw a bunch of ears on a page. Cut them out. These are the ears everyone will use for the game.

Whatever art is created at the party must instantly be included in an art gallery of sorts.

Put out kraft paper on tables so everyone can make a mural together. Other items you can paint together include door hangers or blank tote bags.

Fashion Statement

What better way to say "art" than with a smock, beret, and fun, loud clothes? Wear old clothes or clothes you don't mind getting wrecked.

Good Eats

No art party would be complete without food that requires a smidge of artistic skill. But please ask your parents when using the stove and fondue pots.

Crazy Pizza

Sure, you can make your own pizza in the oven using dough, tomato sauce, and even pepperoni. But you can make a pizza that's a little bit crazier, too. Try some of these wild toppings: beans, broccoli, bell peppers, mushrooms, olives, peanuts, pineapple, carrots, walnuts, sprouts, or salami.

Fancy Fondue

Gather around the fondue pot, everyone! This is the ultimate finger food experience using cheese or chocolate as dips. You need: one genuine fondue pot, food cut into bite-size pieces, cheese or chocolate for melting, and long sticks for dipping. Some perfect dippers: bread cubes (for the cheese), or strawberry, banana, and orange slices (for the chocolate).

Party Treats

Provide tins with crayons or paints/pencil boxes with mini-stickers.

Instead of prizes, give Monopoly money to "buy" art at the end. Go back to your gallery and shop around.

Pass out tins of beads with thread to string them together.

Hot Talk Topics

by Sam and Libby

There is nooo way we're going to have a sleepover and not talk about other people—and one another. There are far too many topics to gossip about, so we've narrowed the list a little bit. Just make sure that no one says anything that would hurt someone's feelings. Even kids who are not at the party! Let the chattering begin!

popularity

nicknames

braces

makeup

being alone

being famous

sweating

being polite

opinionated people

surprises

babysitting

being competitive

working out

gossip

graffiti

growing up

older siblings

moving

guy friends

sharing your room

trading clothes
with friends

cliques

body image

lying to protect
people's feelings

R U Game, Girl?

GAME: Fast Draw

Are you and your BFFs artists? Test yourselves with this quick-drawing game.

> **You need:**
> set of clue cards (blank index cards) • markers
> large board to write on • stopwatch

What to Do:

 Make a set of clue cards. Clues are simply words that indicate an object needing to be drawn (like feathers, moon, or pencil sharpener). Write yours down on the index cards.

2 Divide your sleepover group into two teams.

 Each team sends up a player to draw their version of what's been revealed on a clue card.

 All members of that team are allowed to take guesses about the mystery word. Set a time limit for guessing, like three minutes.

5 All correct guesses are worth one point. The team with the most points at the end of the game...wins!

GAME: Gigglebelly

If you want to crack up nonstop, this is the game for you!

What to Do:

 Have one player lie down on her back. The next player lies down with her head resting on the first player's belly and the next player lies down with her head on the second player's belly. Arrange all the players until everyone is zigzagged around the floor, each with her head on someone else's belly.

 The first player shouts, loud and clear, "Ha!"

 The second player responds with a vigorous, "Ha-ha!"

 The third player says "Ha-ha-ha!" and so on.

 Are you laughing uncontrollably yet? You will be soon!

GAME: Do It Dice

What to Do:

 Ahead of time, find two small square boxes. Paint them white and then write a different command or a stunt on each side of each box. Things like "Recite the Pledge of Allegiance," "Hop up and down on one foot," "Stand on your head," "Say the alphabet backwards," etc.

 Have your friends stand in a big circle.

 The person going first rolls both dice.

 Now she must do what it says on each die – AT THE SAME TIME!

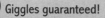 Take turns rolling the dice and performing the stunts.

Giggles guaranteed!

Sleepover Keepsake Ideas

I take pictures of all my friends at slumber parties. I have one photo of Libby when she's sleeping...and I swear she's drooling.

Don't let your party happen without capturing the perfect moments.

- Snap a photo of the whole group decked out in their best pj's.
- Have everyone autograph a page in a blank scrapbook.
- Spend time taking candid pictures during all of the activities. Use a digital camera so you can print out the photos immediately.
- Don't forget those before and after makeover photos!
- Sit together and think about "theme" pages to include in your scrapbook.

1. Girly Girls
2. Song Birds
3. Hobby Time
4. I'm Good At...
5. True Meaning of Friendship
6. Dress Up
7. Hanging Out
8. Athletics
9. Pillow Fight
10. Girl Power

Try a little sleepover graffiti! Just put blank paper (kraft paper) along one wall. Leave out the crayons and markers and watch what gets created.

It's YOUR Party!

Fill in the details of the themes, menu, games, and other plans for your big shindig.

The Friends 4 Ever Top 10

"Things We Just Want to Make Sure You Know Before Having Your Slumber Party" List

1. Invite BFFs only. It's going to be a fun night, but a long night, too, if you're hanging with people you don't know too well.

2. Spend some time making the invitations; and then hand-deliver them to friends. When Rachel did that, we were all so impressed.

3. It isn't geeky to be a super planner for the sleepover. It's smart. Jessie makes charts for everything—including parties. That's why we love her.

4. Must-have: a new pair of pajamas for the occasion. Get thee to a mall, my friend! Libby will meet you there.

5. No boys allowed. That would be weird. This is a girl thing, after all.

6. Noise down after nine o'clock so you don't disturb anyone else in the house. Translation: You don't want the mom and dad of the house coming into your room to say, "Be quiet!" That would be sooo embarrassing.

7. Everyone will probably stay up all night BUT if someone wants to sleep...that's okay, too.

8. Yes, you do have to get up and get going in the morning, so maybe it's a good idea to get some sleep.

9. No pranks. Stay nice. 'Nuff said.

10. When you're curled up in your sleeping bag on the floor next to your best friends in the whole entire world, it's hard not to get a case of the warm fuzzies.

Have a blast planning and enjoying your sleepover. Play right and sleep tight!